The Floofiest Thing

Author: Don Harpell   Illustrator: David Dodson

Published by The Yacky Chicken

Neurodiversity

This book belongs to

_____

ISBN 978-1-998946-07-5

They are gray and they're floofy

like a big teddy bear.

They are cute and cuddly

causing people to stare.

It's not that they are scary

or give people a fright

in fact, as a Squidget

they bring great delight.

They are actually known

as the Floofiest Thing.

They have the softest of fur

in which you sink in.

Much about them is big,

they have the biggest of eyes,

but like a plush teddy bear

they are really fun size.

_____ Taller

_____ fun size

_____ Smaller

They walk into your room,

not to jump on your bed,

but if you ignore them

they might tap your head.

They are not being mean,

they are not being coy,

it is just that they see you

as another fun toy.

Sometimes they jump up.

Sometimes they jump down.

They dive and they duck.

They can be such a clown.

They want you to hurry

there is breakfast to eat.

What will you have for breakfast?

They can't wait to see!

Squidgets always eat healthy,

to make sure they stay well.

They know breakfast is ready,

they can tell by the smell.

They wait near your chair

for you to be done.

They want to get going

to go play and have fun.

Then they jump and they tumble

and scamper about

leaving things in a jumble

before they run out.

What games can be played?

What fun might there be?

So many choices!

Let's go outside and see.

They call for their friends

to come and have fun.

They call for them all,

all together as one.

They do not call names

or keep friends from play.

Even the Weely Garuff

can play in their own way.

The Spotted Uptoo

because they are tall.

The Bobtail Galuff

can juggle some balls.

The Little Brown Shruff

because they are small.

The Weely Garuff

can outrun them all.

When Floofiest plays,

they play with them all.

They love to tell jokes.

They are a funny furry thing.

Their friends all join in

to laugh at the zing.

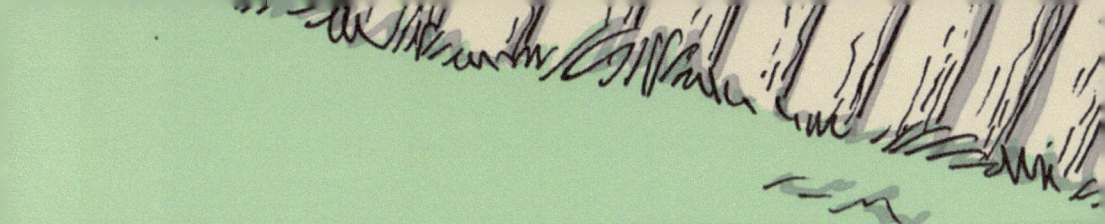

They love dancing music,

and move to the beats,

kept in time by their friends

as they dance up the street.

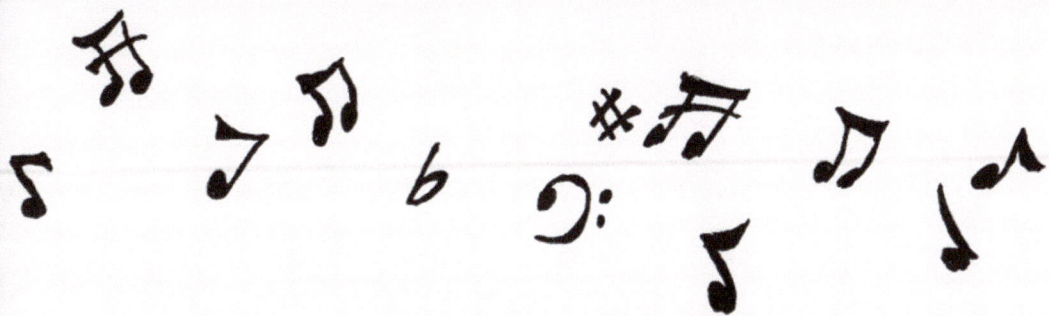

To the playground they go

for more fun things to do.

What do you think of their choice

on the sloopy doop zoom?

Then they went flying

on the long ropey go-high.

And acted like monkeys

on the bars near the slide.

Soon they were warm

and so needed to cool.

To the park full of water

where they swim in the pool.

To the pit full of balls

they decided to go.

Yes, the pit full of balls

with colors of rainbows.

Now home to the backyard,

having shared a good day,

the furriest of friends

end all of their play.

Squidget waves goodbye

to all of their friends,

the Spotted Uptoo,

the Bobtail Galuff,

the Little Brown Shruff and

the Weely Garuff.

They are content, and tired,

and so sit for a meal,

to talk of the day

and how happy they feel.

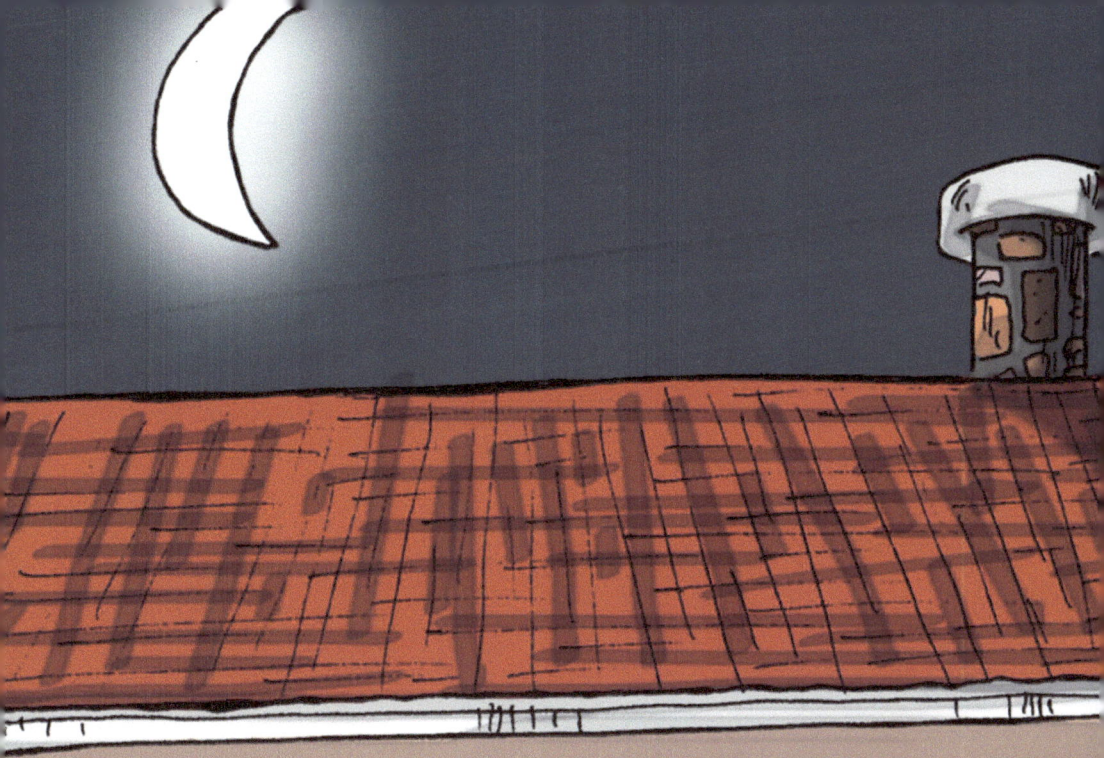

All done their meal,

the day now complete,

they wash up before bed,

so they are ready for sleep.

The sun has gone down

it is time eyes to close,

for Floofiest to dream

while stars twinkle and glow.

Meet the Characters

"Squidget"

Yuki is one of our cats, and we use him in our books. This is his third time in a book. He was first in the Wazoo book, "Squidgets, Wazoos and Wabadeezoos". He still loves food of all kinds and, like his brother Zorro, has taken to eating vegetables. He hopes you eat your vegetables too!

"Wazoo"

Zorro is our older cat who was the main character in the first Wazoo book, "Squidgets, Wazoos and Wabadeezoos". He is a Snowshoe Siamese. They are all love, want to be close and talk all the time. We call him "Z" to shorten his name.

"Weely Garuff"

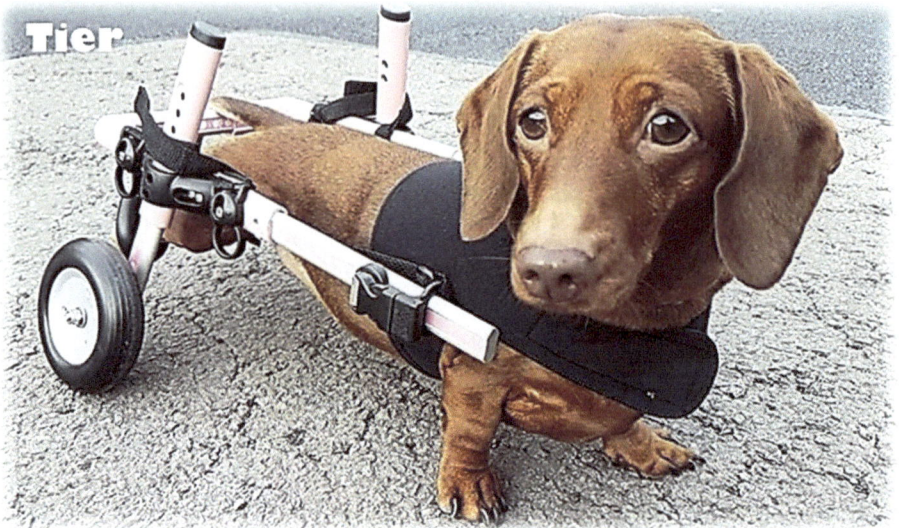

Credit: Nikki & Matt, Dedicated to Dachshunds
https://dedicatedtodachshunds.co.uk/

The dog in the photo is named Tier. She was part of a family, owners Nikki and Matt, who loved Tier with all their heart.

You may see dogs that have four legs and no wheels, but some dogs, their back legs don't work, so they are given wheels – much like a person having a wheelchair. Like the "Weely Garuff", they do not slow down, they are loveable and can be a really good friend.

"Spotted Uptoo"

Credit: Dean King on Instagram
https://www.instagram.com/p/CFCgF3pMHzn

The Spotted Uptoo I based on a cat called a Serval. This picture is of Spartacus, who was adopted from a zoo by a family in Merrimack, New Hampshire. He is very tall and has very bold spots. That's why they are the Spotted Uptoo – because they are tall, have spots and can reach things up high.

"Little Brown Shruff"

Credit: iStockPhoto/igoriss

The Little Brown Shruff is really a hedgehog.
They build their nests in 'hedges' and make
sounds that sound much like a pig. They are
very small. And very cute. Some kids even have
them as pets.

"Bobtail Galuff"

Credit: iStockPhoto/phototrip

Quokka ("kwah-ka") are a happy looking animal. They live in Australia. Their fur is short, fluffy, and brown. They have little round ears and small black noses. They are very friendly!

A Note from The Author

I like having friends who are not just the same as me. Having friends who like what we like is nice, but it is good to see and learn from others. I make friends with people who are taller, shorter, bigger, smaller, or have special needs. Having friends whose body is not the same or may not work the same as mine helps me see the world and how to enjoy it in a much bigger way. I hope you have lots of different friends.

Have fun and enjoy!

www.ingramcontent.com/pod-product-compliance
Lightning Source LLC
LaVergne TN
LVHW010029070426
835511LV00004B/96